The Mother of All Journeys

D1333637

The Mother of All Journeys

Coming to Terms With Having a Baby

Helen Bells

authorHOUSE®

AuthorHouse™
1663 Liberty Drive
Bloomington, IN 47403
www.authorhouse.com
Phone: 1-800-839-8640

© 2012 by Helen Bells. All rights reserved.

No part of this book may be reproduced, stored in a retrieval system, or transmitted by any means without the written permission of the author.

First published by AuthorHouse   March 2012

ISBN: 978-1-4567-9729-4 (sc)
ISBN: 978-1-4567-9730-0 (ebk)

Printed in the United States of America

Front cover design by Clare Scott.

This book is printed on acid-free paper.

Because of the dynamic nature of the Internet, any web addresses or links contained in this book may have changed since publication and may no longer be valid. The views expressed in this work are solely those of the author and do not necessarily reflect the views of the publisher, and the publisher hereby disclaims any responsibility for them.

For my husband, family and friends -
thank you for being there for me, unconditionally

Contents

A NOTE FROM THE AUTHOR

I wish someone had told me that I might not enjoy being a mother, that there would be times I would feel like a failure, that I might hate my "new" life, but nobody did.

Before I start, I would just like to state, for the record, that I love my son very much and I wouldn't change him for the world. He makes me laugh and smile (now) and he is an absolute treasure, so no need for anyone to call Social Services and declare me unfit to raise a child.

Right then, the million dollar question: *why am I bothering to write all this?* There are several answers. Firstly, I thought it would be therapeutic to write down my innermost thoughts and feelings to try to make some sense of them. Secondly, my friends and family encouraged me to share my experiences by writing a book that may help others who are having difficulty coming to terms with pregnancy / motherhood. And lastly, I felt it would be a serious personal achievement writing anything this lengthy!

There are so many books out there that are medically factual (I can't compete with these as I am not qualified in that department) and so many others that simply paint a picture of a blissful world with bump and then baby (I can't do that either, it didn't happen) and I feel people deserve to know that having a baby is not always fantastic and not necessarily the best thing in the world. Maybe for some, but not for me.

That's it in a nutshell. I did not enjoy pregnancy or being a full time mum and looking after a baby, something I suspect many mothers feel although are afraid to say. By writing down my true feelings about how I found impending motherhood and motherhood itself and by sharing them, I hope other people may be able to relate to them and realise they are not misfits, they are not abnormal in feeling that having a child has not made their life complete.

I like to go along with the view of Karen Horney, a German psychoanalyst and psychiatrist who said "the perfect normal person is rare in our civilization", but of course if there is nobody out there who does feel the same as me or can associate with what I have written, then I must truly be a freak of nature.

LIFE
BEFORE
BABY

1

FROM SLIM AND TRIM TO FRUMPY AND GRUMPY

We decided we wanted a baby, my husband Duncan and I.

We had been married for one and half years and weren't getting any younger - no time like the present. Mid thirties were fast approaching for me and dare I say it, late thirties for Duncan. In my mind I had always seen forty as the cut off point for women having babies, so it was logical to me that we start trying for a child as we were both realistic it could take months if not years. We decided we wouldn't actively try to conceive. None of this measuring temperatures, counting the days, taking special tablets, having sex non-stop; we just carried on our lives as normal, not really giving it another thought.

Not giving another thought that is, until I fell asleep at the beauty therapist's one afternoon whilst having a pedicure. It wasn't the first time I had felt utterly exhausted that week and I couldn't understand why I was acting like a zombie. Although I like my sleep, this was totally abnormal even by my standards. And then the light slowly started to dawn.

I drove home at a snail's pace, thinking about the possibility of being pregnant but definitely not expecting I would be, as it had only been a month since we had stopped using contraception. I dragged my feet up the three flights of stairs to our flat and I can picture it now: me home alone, taking a pregnancy test in our sunny bathroom, seeing the positive result, having to sit down to steady myself and taking another test, just to make sure. Disbelief. The result was still the same.

But there was no jumping for joy, no feelings of elation, nothing. I had expected to be over the moon, bursting with happiness and excitement, bouncing up and down with delight but none of it came. The reality was I had to go and lie down in our bedroom and take deep breaths to deal with the panic that was slowly rising, with not even a glass of vino to calm my nerves.

I had no idea how to tell Duncan, whether to call him at work or whether to take him somewhere special for dinner. So in the end I decided I would leave the positive result for him to see on the side in the bathroom. I can picture his reaction as clearly as mine: a state of shock and having to pour himself a large glass of whisky.

The truth is we didn't expect it to happen so quickly and were totally surprised. I had definitely thought it would be a matter of months and couldn't believe this was it. I was going to be a mother, Duncan was going to be a father, we were going to have a baby, and we were pregnant. And when I say we were pregnant, I do mean WE were pregnant. Duncan went through everything with me during those nine months. I would say the good and the bad but I don't really remember there being much good, right from the beginning.

I should have been delighted that we had conceived so quickly. It doesn't happen to everyone and it was what we wanted wasn't it? Yes. Was I overjoyed with the prospect of having a baby and starting a family? No. It filled me with dread and occasionally horror, strange feelings for someone who is generally a gregarious, positive, happy and outgoing person who loves children. I kept these feelings away from Duncan as I didn't want to put a dampener on things. I tried to convince myself I was excited and that I couldn't wait to be a mother, my theory being that the more I told myself this, the more I would hear it, the more I would believe it and then somehow the more I would feel it. But it didn't work.

We decided to tell people our "great" news in person before the usual twelve weeks - I am hopeless at keeping secrets. So we went on a spree of visiting the extended family. Each time I burst into tears without fail, telling myself and everyone else they were tears of joy, although they were actually tears of trepidation, tears for life as I knew it being over. Things would never be the same, there was no going back. I tried to tell myself to man up, to pull myself together, but it didn't work. I really couldn't understand why I felt like this and was so frustrated not to feel more positive and excited.

Gradually I found my unhappiness too hard to hide and it soon became obvious to Duncan, especially as I always use him as a sounding block for my thoughts and feelings. Why was I so down in the dumps when I had everything to live for? I had a loving, caring husband, ditto for my family, and a great network of friends. Why was I sad? I had no idea. I felt I was going mad and was losing sight of my life as I spiralled downwards away from reality. Although Duncan was reassuring, we didn't tell anyone else how I felt because I thought they would consider me a weirdo, an odd-bod in society, a misfit, rather like a leper.

I borrowed and bought books on being pregnant and having babies and devoured them all, cover to cover, even making notes. Each week I would give Duncan a little summary of what was happening inside me and we would read excerpts from books together but it still didn't seem real. I still couldn't quite believe it. I was also hoping to find something somewhere to which I could relate, so I could know I was human after all and that other people had felt like me. But there was nothing and it made me feel even more abnormal.

Bedtime was awful from the start. I couldn't sleep, I tossed and turned, I felt claustrophobic, I was too hot, too cold. I hated having Duncan anywhere near me and the bed felt tiny, far too small for the two (or three) of us. At times I was so cross and so tired that I took myself off into the spare room to try to calm down. After a while I went back into our bed, feeling more in control and less like tearing out my hair and screaming with anger. I had never had problems sleeping before and I found it extremely difficult when I was suddenly faced with this. Somebody suggested natural sleeping tablets which were definitely a help and allowed me to get a better night's rest.

When we went for our first scan I was secretly holding out that this would be a turning point and that suddenly I would see our baby on the screen and everything would fall into place and I would be happy. I had visions of myself smiling, being a radiant, expectant mother, blooming, taking everything in my stride and being in control of myself again. But sadly it wasn't to be. As I lay on the bed at the hospital with the cold gel on my tummy, Duncan tightly holding my hand, looking at the screen at our baby, I didn't feel anything. Nothing. No emotion. Nothing. I was so let down by myself. What sort of human being was I? I felt as though I was a monster, looking at our child and not caring. We bought photos of the scan and I kept one in my wallet to show people, again hoping that this would somehow kick start my maternal feelings. But to no avail.

Lots of my friends had had babies before me and I recall them being perfect mothers to be: cool, calm, collected and above all positive. I constantly wondered why I didn't feel the same and thought about how I could make myself feel like them. Why couldn't I be even a little bit enthusiastic, was it too much to ask? Whenever I smiled it was generally a veneer, masking the fact that I wasn't actually looking forward to having a baby, that at times I even wished we weren't having a baby.

I remember a relative kindly phoning up to see how our first scan had gone and in my honest fashion I told her that I didn't want to have the baby and would prefer to leave it at the hospital when it was born. Not particularly nice but honest. There was no escaping the fact that things weren't getting better and despite everyone's kindness and support, I couldn't envisage them improving,

I can't remember exactly when it was but there was one good weekend when I really tried to make an effort and enjoy myself. We were going to a friend's father's 60th birthday party in Herefordshire, and whilst I wasn't particularly eager about having to be sociable and the prospect of dancing didn't fill me with joy, I was looking forward to going away and having a break. Duncan had booked a B&B on a working farm and it couldn't have been more tranquil and relaxing: we were surrounded by fields and hills, not a house in sight, just the smell of the animals and the farm, heaven. We left the party quite early as I was tired as ever, and I relished lying on pristinely clean sheets, in a different room, in someone else's house, with the prospect of a full English breakfast being cooked for me the next day.

Not long after this, things gradually seemed to worsen. It was not just my mental state I had to contend with, by now often on a daily basis, but my physical state too. After a dinner party in Oxford with some friends, I woke up the next day and started to feel nauseous almost immediately. We even had to stop twice on the car journey home because I felt the need to be sick. And that was how my morning sickness was until the second half of the pregnancy: the feeling of a permanent hangover that just wouldn't shift, never actually being sick but feeling like I needed to be, 24/7.

"Operation anti-morning-sickness" was put into place. The air fresheners around the house and in the car had to be removed and I had to take a sick bag with me everywhere. I went to the doctor and was prescribed medication which did nothing. I still felt I needed to be by a bucket at all times, and this was one more thing to make me dislike the baby I was carrying and begrudge its existence even more.

The only good thing was food. My life started to revolve around it to get me through the day. I took time off work because it was all I could do to walk from the bedroom to the bathroom. However after a while I decided I just had to get on with it. I couldn't stay at home in bed all the time or life would pass me by. I remember a normal weekday would be having breakfast before leaving for work, stopping at McDonald's for breakfast number two before reaching work, having a large mid-morning snack at work, eating a large lunch in the canteen, getting home in time for tea by myself and then eating dinner with my husband when he got home. Food glorious food.

One of the few social engagements I accepted at this time was a rather special invitation from my father who was receiving an OBE at Buckingham Palace. I had my fingers crossed that the morning sickness would have passed by the time the grand occasion arrived and I wouldn't draw attention to myself with a public display of illness. The books all say that morning sickness generally clears by about twelve weeks but for twelve read twenty. It just went on and on and on. When my father's big day finally arrived I sat near the back of the room, discreetly eating a large packet of Jelly Babies in an attempt to curb the nausea - ready to dash out if necessary. Luckily I didn't disgrace myself in front of Prince Charles but it was certainly an hour or two of fist and jaw clenching!

Not surprisingly, I started to put on weight and this was another factor I found very hard to deal with. I had been used to being a petite size 8 and suddenly I couldn't do up any of my trousers or skirts. This was particularly frustrating since my friend Charlotte had recently had a baby and wore her normal jeans throughout her pregnancy, looking slim and slinky even when she was about to pop.

Friends lent me maternity clothes and I bought a couple of items on-line. This made me feel a bit better because firstly it meant I could try to disguise the bump and secondly, wearing clothes that actually did up didn't make me feel quite so fat, frumpy and revolting. I couldn't believe Duncan still found me attractive but he constantly told me he did and I think he meant it. He was so loving and caring, despite the fact his wife had turned into a person he probably didn't recognise, both in body and mind.

My friend Karen came round one night after work and she had actually travelled quite a distance especially to see me. She brought some ginger tea to try to help the sickness and she had prepared a delicious meal, a fantastic South African dish with mincemeat, mango chutney and egg, a real hit. I don't think I was much company but it was nice to know that my friends still counted me as a friend, despite me being such a rubbish one in return.

2

THINGS CAN ONLY GET BETTER

I can't remember exactly how many weeks pregnant I was when we went for our second scan but this was the one where you can find out the sex of the baby if you want to. I wanted to as I hoped this would make me feel closer to the thing growing inside me, that I would see it as a person, not an encumbrance. But Duncan didn't. Slight problem. We resolved the situation by deciding I would find out the sex of the baby and not tell a single soul, not even my parents or sister - a potentially hard task, considering we are a close and open family - and Duncan would leave the room whilst I was told.

So once again we found ourselves in Guildford hospital in the room where I had lain previously, staring at the monitor without any feelings. Would this time be different? I fervently hoped so. I just wanted things to be back to normal, to make things better not only for myself, so I could feel like a human being again, but equally for Duncan, so he didn't have to come home each day to a wife who was feeling sorry for herself and slowly falling apart.

Looking at the screen, we could see we had a healthy baby, for which I was most relieved. When the moment came to find out the sex, Duncan left the room and I was told we were going to be having a little boy. I remember crying and crying. Not with joy and delight unfortunately, more likely because it was confirmed I did have a baby in me, but at least I had some emotion and wasn't devoid of all feeling, as I had believed I was those days. I was pleased we were going to have a boy for Duncan's sake as I knew that secretly he wanted a son. I just wished I could have told him and we could have shared the news together. I like doing things together and this made me feel even more alone.

Because Duncan didn't know the sex of the baby, we decided to refer to it in the masculine form and we named it "Junkanoo" after our honeymoon experience in the Bahamas (their version of Mardi Gras is known as "Junkanoo", a word we found really funny). Now the baby had a name of sorts and I knew the sex, I did actually start to feel I was bonding with it and no longer felt I wanted to leave it at the hospital when it was born. I still wasn't enamoured with the idea of having a baby or relishing the prospect of looking after it, but it definitely helped knowing we were going to have a little boy.

Amongst all my negativity and wallowing in self-pity, I do remember one exciting moment that still makes me smile fondly, and think lovingly of the baby we had made which was half me and half Duncan. Driving back from some friends' house one Sunday afternoon, I had this funny feeling in my tummy and had no idea what it was. It was like a fluttering of butterfly wings and it wasn't trapped wind. It was the baby moving! It was such an amazing feeling and I think this was the first bit of optimism I had that things might turn out OK in the end. Not surprisingly at this stage of the pregnancy, Duncan wasn't able to feel the movement although I couldn't wait until he would be able to.

Throughout the pregnancy, this was one thing that never ceased to amaze me, the movement of a tiny life inside me. It was only a few weeks after this momentous occasion of feeling the foetus move that Duncan actually felt our little baby move too. After this, whenever it moved and Duncan was there, I always wanted him to put his hand on my tummy to feel it, so we could share it and have a bit of peaceful togetherness. I think this was the best part of being pregnant, feeling the baby move inside me and knowing that we had created it.

With tangible evidence of this new life, we bought a book of baby names, again to try and make impending motherhood seem real for me and to try and share some excitement and enthusiasm. We did actually have a laugh doing this every so often in the weeks that ensued as some of the names were simply so ridiculous to us that we couldn't believe anyone in their right mind would choose them for a child - although I did want to name our child Paddington so I'm a fine one to talk! We even took the book out to a Dunkin Doughnuts café in

Guildford, where we scoffed a selection of twelve of their finest whilst simultaneously scoffing at some of the more obscure names. Anyway, after much discussion, we decided our favourite names for a boy were David or Daniel and we couldn't settle on anything for a girl - not a problem for us though as I knew we were having a boy.

With Christmas coming up, Duncan and I decided we would treat ourselves to an expensive five star holiday in Mexico, our last "just the two of us" holiday. Maybe with some sunshine and relaxation things would improve and I would start to feel positive about our future with a baby. Sadly, it didn't work out quite as planned. Whilst I had a lovely time relaxing by the pool and the sea, I was still feeling nauseous and just looked fat in my bikini, as if I had eaten too many pies. I hated people seeing my body. I had always looked alright on the beach and now I looked like a beached whale.

I remember clearly one night, hiding in the bed under the covers and telling Duncan I wished I had a coat hanger and a bottle of vodka as I hated the baby so much I wanted to get rid of it. I knew this must have been heart-breaking for him but I couldn't help how I felt. I could hear myself saying these awful words and I was totally unable to do anything about it. I wish I felt differently but I didn't. I thought I was the worst expectant mother in the world, heartless and cruel, and this made me feel guilty and even worse about myself.

Duncan was supportive and patient the whole time but things came to a crunch on New Year's Eve. After all, he had feelings and emotions too and who was there for him? I could barely focus on anything other than myself and was totally self-consumed in my sadness and loathing of life, leaving him to pick up the pieces as well as try to be happy for the two of us. So it should have come as no surprise when he simply shut down and said he didn't want to go out or see in the New Year with me on our balcony watching fireworks.

I found him instead sitting in the bathroom crying his heart out. I felt terrible for him, not knowing what to do. It was the first time I had ever seen him cry and it really shocked me. It made me realise that we were in it together, that I was not alone in my grief, that we needed to look after each other, that marriage is give and take, not just take take take on my part. But whilst this probably made us a slightly more cohesive unit, unfortunately things still did not really improve for me.

When we got home I went back to work and I had to put on the façade of happiness and positivity. There was another member of staff at school who was pregnant too and she always looked fantastic, tottering around in her little skin-tight outfits and high heels while I felt ugly and wanted to curl up in a ball, to go to sleep and never wake up. I couldn't be honest and open with anyone and tell them how I felt as I assumed they would think I was some sort of psycho who shouldn't be allowed to bring a child into this world. This went on, day after day, week after week, and all I could see was doom and gloom. I couldn't even have a bottle of pink fizz to escape it all.

Having said this, looking back I do remember there were some little things every now and then that pierced my darkness with a sunbeam, tiny glimmers of hope that made me realise I was maybe not a lost cause. Perhaps I could somehow rejoin the human race in the not too distant future . . .

At one of the seemingly many check-ups with a midwife, I remember her asking if I would like to hear the baby's heartbeat. Although I didn't think I would care to, I did listen to the heartbeat and it was absolutely amazing. This noise rather like a horse galloping through a field, its hooves pounding against the ground, was our baby! It was our little Junkanoo, a person, who needed me to nurture it and love it, not hate it.

Another moment of excitement for both of us was actually seeing the baby kick when looking at my tummy, not just feeling it with a hand placed there. It was hard to believe there was a little adventurer inside me, bursting with energy and trying to get out to play with us and have cuddles.

But this novelty did start to wear off after a while in as much as the Junkanoo would kick for most of the night and make it even more uncomfortable to sleep than it already was. Now, although I wasn't looking forward to having a baby, I couldn't wait to get it out.

After what seemed like an eternity, one day I woke up and didn't recognise myself - I didn't feel sick anymore! I couldn't believe my luck, finally! It was such a relief and I immediately crossed my fingers that this would be the beginning of the new "phase" in my pregnancy. Alas, it was not to be. That very night, as I lay in bed trying to go to sleep, I had this burning feeling in my chest and thought it must be on fire. I had no idea what was happening but I felt dreadful once again with no power to do anything about it.

I phoned up a doctor friend, Jo, and she told me it was heartburn. I had seen adverts for remedies to this ailment on television, never having any idea what they were about, but now I knew exactly what they were talking about. Duncan was rapidly dispatched to pick up something to make me feel better. From that day until Junkanoo was born, I carried an extra-large bottle of Gaviscon around with me. I didn't even bother with a spoon but swigged straight from the bottle when I needed to relive the pain. If I'd had shares in the company I would have been rich!

3

THE BEGINNING OF THE END

The next milestones in my pregnancy were maternity leave and moving house, the former happening because of the latter and both occurring simultaneously. I was really hopeful that stopping work might help me become more like my old self, as there would be less on my plate and less to worry about.

We moved house in the April with my husband's job when I was 29 weeks pregnant, so this seemed like the sensible time to stop work and start making a new home for our baby. The plan was for me to get to know the area, make some friends and get things ready in our house, exactly how we wanted them to be for our little addition. Thankfully, the last trimester was a big improvement on the first two.

The first thing I did was look at local groups I could join, antenatal ones if possible as I thought it would be sensible to meet some other women locally in the same situation as me. As I have said, I've always been an outgoing person who enjoys meeting people so I found it odd and

19

frightening when I was filled with dread at the prospect of having to make new friends and join new classes.

My good university friend Nikki suggested I join a local NCT group but I really didn't find this idea appealing. The thought of sitting around drinking coffee or tea (and eating biscuits and becoming even fatter), and either having to lie through gritted teeth about how wonderful being pregnant was or tell the truth about how awful I had found everything and feeling I would be treated like an outcast, was not good. I had no desire to share my feelings with people I didn't know, just because we happened to be expectant mothers. Thankfully Nikki was sensitive enough and kind enough not to push it. I knew she was trying to help and I knew she enjoyed these coffee mornings herself.

I spent a while trawling the Web - what a great invention - for local classes and finally came up with the idea of antenatal yoga. I have never been into yoga or anything that doesn't require raising the heartbeat and getting sweaty, but as I could barely walk to the top of our road without collapsing in a heap I thought this would be a good idea. It would kill two birds with one stone: meeting people and getting some exercise.

I remember turning up at my first class and the instructor, Jessica, was so lovely and empathetic. I was slightly taken aback, though, when we didn't launch straight into some yoga moves and she went around the room asking everyone how their week had been. Whilst people mentioned all the physical symptoms they were experiencing, nobody mentioned anything else. I was hoping somebody might say they were not looking forward to having a baby so I wouldn't feel like the only one who was different, but nobody did and I still felt like an alien in human form.

The yoga classes were great and I began to look forward to them. Whilst I was no expert and would certainly not be hanging out at the local Hare Krishna Temple, I enjoyed this time for me where I had nothing to think about, nothing to worry about and could switch off and relax.

I didn't make any friends though. I had this vision in my mind of getting on with everybody, as I would have once upon a time, and it just wasn't like that. People were friendly but that was it. I guess their lives were busy. They had lived in the area for ages and already had their circle of friends. I had heard stories of pregnant women who became friends at antenatal classes and kept in touch even when their children were grown up, and this is what I wanted to happen to me. But it didn't. Not straight away at any rate.

I also seemed a bit of a fraud in as much as everyone else at yoga was still working, even those who were nearly full term. I felt ridiculous saying that I had stopped working, as if I was some lazy, good-for-nothing "lady what lunches". I had thought I would love being on maternity leave and that doing nothing and being able to swan around leading a life of leisure would be great fun but the reality was very different. I found my new existence meaningless and my day to day life became empty. Duncan would go off to work and I would be by myself. I started to question my self-worth, what was the point of my existence? I contributed nothing to our family life at home, I didn't bring in any money, I was miserable the majority of the time, I was fat and ugly with cellulite down past my knees, I had gone off sex completely, what sort of life was this? Not a life I wanted to lead, that was for sure.

One day I was in the local library (mixing with the local community being another thing on my moving house hit list). As I was glancing at the local ads on my way out I saw a flyer for a local walking group which met every Thursday morning. Right up my street, metaphorically and almost literally. I decided I would be brave and turned up by myself the next day, which happened to be a Thursday. It must have been fate. To say everyone was rather old would be an understatement. I was the youngest there by far, but people were polite to me and some chatted to me and looked like they enjoyed my company. I went back the following week, and the week after that. My "OAP Walk" as I called it was firmly put onto my social calendar.

From that moment, wherever I went locally, it seemed as if I bumped into someone from the walking group! One sunny day I was treating myself to lunch al fresco in a local café and a lady I didn't recognise popped over and said hello, that she recognised me from the walk and that her name was Wendy. That was it. The moment was over in a flash, almost like a day-dream. But it made me feel special and it made me feel part of life, however momentary.

On a particular walk in May, Bernard, one of the leaders, made an announcement that he had some baby tomato plants he had not managed to sell at the local church fête and if anybody would like some, they were welcome to go round to his house after the walk and collect them. Unfortunately I spent too long in the café afterwards and missed Bernard to ask him directions to his house, so Maureen, one of the other leaders, offered to take me there in her car and drop me home afterwards. This gesture really touched me and I realised that people do care, that they are kind, that I am not alone and that I should try to stop feeling sorry for myself, although this was definitely easier said than done.

Another thing I did when we moved house was to look up baby classes for Junkanoo. I wanted to give him all the best starts in life, let him try as many different things as possible, for him to be a well-cared-for and nurtured child. I drew up a spread sheet (I love spread sheets) with possible activities for each day of the week that we could do together. I then made my selection:

Monday	Baby weigh in and toy library
Tuesday	Baby swimming
Wednesday	Baby yoga (with Jessica, obviously)
Thursday	Baby signing
Friday	Baby massage

At least I still had the ability to be practical and forward plan, or be neurotic and anal, depends how you look at it. One big problem was revealed though when I called up to enlist the Junkanoo in these classes: they only ran during term time. No good to me when Junkanoo was going to be born in the middle of the summer. I panicked about what I was going to do. I couldn't face the prospect of having no goal to my day. It was bad enough having to entertain only myself for a whole day while Duncan was at work, let alone a baby as well.

Naturally I also registered with the local doctors' surgery and the new midwife suggested I go on a one day antenatal class at the local hospital with other pregnant mothers. I clung to this as much as I had clung to every other straw, hoping that somehow this would be the day I would have an epiphany and the light would dawn that we were having a baby and that everything was going to be great.

Duncan and I also decided it would be a good idea to get Junkanoo's room ready, to try to get excited together and start to see ourselves as a little family. I have to say I did enjoy doing this, organising, sorting, and getting everything just right. I put some things for him into the chest of drawers we had bought. Duncan put up pictures and we made up the new cot with toys and bedding. We even had a blanket that used to belong to Duncan when he was a baby - his mother had kept it all these years. I enjoyed going into the room to look at it and would often imagine the Junkanoo in there. Every time I walked up the stairs, the first thing I would see was Duncan's blanket as Junkanoo's room was directly opposite at the end of the landing. Things were starting to improve and I felt I was finally coming to terms with having a baby.

The day of the antenatal class at Watford General Hospital was boiling and whilst Duncan and I didn't particularly learn any relevant new information - we had obviously absorbed everything from the books, top students - it was an opportunity to look around the hospital and familiarise ourselves with the surroundings. This was where I would be in a couple of weeks. I couldn't believe it. Only a couple of weeks. Me, with a baby. OMG. OMG.

It must be a Government initiative but throughout the pregnancy, breast feeding was pushed upon me by everyone and everything: all the leaflets, all the pamphlets, all the books, all the brochures, all the DVDs, all the posters - is my point coming across?

I wouldn't have minded so much if an educated discussion / debate had been put forward for both sides of the story but it came across that if you didn't breast feed then you weren't normal and might be arrested for such a heinous crime. Duncan and I decided that I would give it a go and if it didn't work out, then so be it. I wasn't going to beat myself up about it.

My friend Nikki by now had realised I had found pregnancy hard work and came round to see me one day, bringing lots of clothes with her that her little boy had outgrown. She was so kind and came around with bags and bags of goodies, mostly from her but some from a friend of hers who had had two boys who she dressed in expensive and rather nice clothes. I looked through them all and then stashed them in the cupboard upstairs so that Duncan wouldn't see them and therefore know the sex of the baby. I would just have to wash them very early on a really sunny day, quickly get them out on the line to dry and have them folded and put away by the time Duncan returned from work - easy.

That evening Duncan asked how my day had been but rather than saying something sensible like "oh, you know, the usual" and not giving the game away, I launched into a full account of my day with Nikki as I was actually feeling good about things and thought Duncan would be delighted with my enthusiasm. Unfortunately, when the words "it's such a good thing Nikki has a little baby boy who will be a few months older than Junkanoo as we can have all his cast-offs" were uttered, there was no going back and I had well and truly given the game away after months of secrecy. I couldn't believe it. I was so cross with myself and disappointed that Duncan had found out because I knew he was keen for it to be a surprise. On the flip side though, at least it was a little boy like he wanted!

My two great university friends, Van and Laura, also went out of their way to include me and booked the three of us into a local spa for a weekend. Although I was seriously pregnant by this stage and wouldn't be able to make full use of all the facilities, I could relax and get away from it all, some final "me" time before the arrival of the Junkanoo. Looking back, my friends were so kind to me and this too was hard for me to accept, as I was not a particularly fun person to be around and I couldn't understand why they bothered themselves with me.

One evening during a yoga class, Jessica mentioned that she did private lessons for expectant couples in their home. I jumped at the prospect and couldn't wait to get home and mention this to Duncan to see what he would think. Not surprisingly, he wasn't quite as up for it as I was. I might even go as far as saying he was a little sceptical, but by this stage in the pregnancy, anything that would possibly make me happier that wouldn't break the bank, he was keen to try.

So we enlisted Jessica's help for a couple of hours the Sunday afternoon before the due date, 21st June

2009. She turned up with one of those large exercise balls and spent the session showing the two of us how we could use what I had learnt in yoga to help me through labour. I was so relieved that Duncan was being shown these things too as this meant he would be able to help when the day actually came. I think he considered the money could have been better spent on other things but the private session with Jessica made me feel I was ready to face whatever was coming my way and whilst I might find it awful, at least I could take steps myself to do something about it. For the first time in ages I felt I could do it, that I would get through it, that we would manage and we would tackle whatever was sent our way.

One thing I also thought I should focus on to try to boost my self-esteem before having the Junkanoo was my personal appearance. I didn't want to be in hospital, surrounded by people - doctors, nurses, midwives, friends, relatives, you name them - and look totally dreadful. Slightly dreadful was only to be expected I decided, but anything I could do beforehand to give me a fighting chance of looking decent in preparation for the big day was a must. I duly therefore booked myself into the hairdresser's to have my hair done, the nail salon to have a pedicure (no point anyone trying to do anything with my fingernails, they are always so bitten and picked there is not really much to work with) and the beauty salon to have my eyebrows and lashes tinted and waxed. It was as near to beautiful as I was going to get and I was then ready to have a baby!

The due date came and went, not surprisingly for a first child so everyone told me, and I was becoming more and more impatient, desperate for this baby to make an appearance as I had had enough and the weather was sweltering. Duncan and I tried to do things to keep us occupied and we went to see "Les Misérables" at the theatre one night which was as brilliant as always. Junkanoo clearly enjoyed it too as he kicked his way through the whole thing even if he wasn't in time to the music. At the bus stop on the way home a lady started chatting to me and I recognised her as a lady from the OAP walk although I didn't know her name. We conversed for a few minutes and then went our separate ways and I thought how friendly the people were around our new local area and how joining the walking group had been a good thing for me to do.

We also decided we would book a holiday for when the Junkanoo was born to give ourselves something to look forward to. We bought tickets to fly to Bordeaux as we thought it would be a perfect, low-key holiday to go and visit my parents at their house in France. This would give us time to get a passport for Junkanoo and then we would go on our first family get-away. Hooray!

Nearly a week after the due date I was becoming more and more uncomfortable and coping badly. I couldn't sleep. I couldn't get comfy. I was so cumbersome, it was a drag. We had been trying all the usual things to bring about labour (curry, sex etc.) but to no avail. My mother suggested going for reflexology and her local reflexologist looked up someone in my area who specialised in reflexology to induce labour. We thought we would give it a shot and if it didn't work, well, at least I would have had a foot massage! The session itself lasted a couple of hours and was actually quite painful, more painful than a normal session, that's for sure. I booked another appointment for two days' time, in case Junkanoo hadn't put in an appearance by then, and went home to see what might happen. Oh yes, and I drank nearly four mouthfuls of castor oil, something Duncan assured me would bring about labour.

Whether it was the reflexology, the special drink or neither of the aforementioned I shall never know, but that evening at around nine o'clock I went into labour. This coincided with terrible diarrhoea and the hugest pain around my bottom - either a haemorrhoid the size of a large battery or a prolapsed bowel. But that is by the by and whichever it was it continues to give me problems.

The following morning on Sunday 28th June, after a night of being awake and in serious pain, our little Junkanoo, David, was finally born in Watford General Hospital. I had warned Duncan I might not want him placed on me immediately as I was unsure how I would feel towards him but it was love at first sight. This was such a relief for me, that I loved our child and had motherly feelings, that I felt protective over him and would do anything for him, that it was real, true, unconditional love. As I lay on the table in the theatre and they sewed up the episiotomy, I cried and cried. All the horrible words I had said, all the nasty thoughts I had had, the emotional roller coaster I had been on over the last nine months, the different person I had been, it was over and I was a mother. Duncan and I were proud parents of a healthy little boy.

LIFE
AFTER
BABY

4

ALL THINGS GROW WITH LOVE

I won't dwell on the hospital experience as it was probably pretty similar to lots of other people's: I was in a ward with various other mothers and babies. I couldn't stop looking at Junkanoo in his cot next to me and I couldn't believe that it had really happened, that we had a baby. The only awful incident apart from giving birth was losing control of my bowel on the midwife when she was helping me shower and it going all over her and the floor. I was mortified and wondered if nappies came in adult size.

Family came and went. It was all a bit of a haze as I hadn't slept for an eternity and I was so exhausted. I was not totally with it and I actually think I had an outer-body experience, everything was so surreal. After a bit of sleep though, I looked forward with trepidation to the day we could take home our new baby and start doing things as a family.

The day we left the hospital I found it very difficult to walk due to my sore bottom and the stitches, a fantastic combination and I wasn't sure which hurt more. Duncan had taken two weeks' paternity leave so we drove home, at a snail's pace and avoiding the bumps where possible, ready to settle into our new life.

Initially it was nothing but feeding the Junkanoo, literally. He would feed, need to be burped, sleep, feed, need to be burped, sleep, with the occasional bath thrown in for good measure. Breast-feeding was excruciatingly painful and exhausting but it was amazing to see this little thing needing me and relying on me. With Duncan at home things were good: he could keep on top of the housework, prepare the meals, look after us, in fact, do everything that I couldn't do and normally did. He was a star. We would just look at David sleeping in his cot, standing there staring, like a couple of star-struck teenagers, holding hands and smiling at each other.

The novelty of breastfeeding soon wore off. Every time Duncan passed David to me to be fed, literally every 1 ½ hours, I would feel like crying and often did. All I saw of David was him attached to my breast and nothing else. It was taking its toll on me and I didn't want my only time with him to be spent in agony. We discussed bottle-feeding but decided I would try to stick to breastfeeding for as long as possible, after all, "breast is best" and don't forget it.

About five days after Junkanoo was born, very early one morning, I noticed blood in his sick. I woke Duncan to have a look and check I wasn't imagining things and as the doctors' surgery was closed we phoned the hospital and they suggested we took David in to be looked at. We rushed in, concerned new parents, terrified that it was something awful, but luckily the blood was only from my nipples and David was fine. This news was such a relief. I had been so worried about our little baby and had felt so helpless at not being able to do anything. I did find it strange, though, that bleeding nipples hadn't been mentioned in any of the baby books I had read - the first of many things that books about having a baby had neglected to mention.

Whilst in hospital I took the opportunity to mention to a midwife that I was thinking about stopping breastfeeding but all she had to say was "every mother can breastfeed and if it hurts then she's not doing it properly". I wanted to clobber her there and then. I couldn't believe my ears. Whilst in the post natal ward I had asked three experts in the hospital on different occasions to check I was doing things properly and they had all agreed I was, so her comment was unbelievable. This was just the sort of talk I didn't need to hear. It made me feel really badly about myself and the seeds of doubt that I was any good as a mother were planted in my mind.

The next day we decided to give Junkanoo formula milk. I cannot describe how relieved I felt when we had decided this. I could share the feeds with Duncan and I could enjoy watching David as he fed, a win-win situation. I did feel guilty and selfish though, worrying if I was doing the right thing.

To celebrate David being one week old and the fact that I was healing, albeit still looking pregnant, we went out to a local tea room for a light lunch. It was such a lovely occasion for Duncan and me as everyone admired little David and said how gorgeous he was. I was delighted and so proud it made me feel all warm inside.

We received cards and presents from so many people wishing us all the best and congratulating us, even people we didn't know especially well or hadn't seen in years. People were thrilled for us and I was thrilled too. It was heart-warming and touching.

One afternoon we decided to be adventurous and walk up the road from our house to get out and have some fresh air. In the final stages of my pregnancy this amble had been exhausting and very hard work - it's a very steep hill - taking me about ten minutes to get to the top when it took a person of average fitness about four. So there we were, slowly making our way to the top with the push chair, when this lady in a red car zoomed by and then screeched to a halt. She reversed a bit and we saw it was the lady from the OAP walk whom we had met at the bus stop after "Les Misérables". She flagged us down and handed over a present for David. How kind when I had only spoken to her once and didn't even know her name! She explained she hadn't been driving the streets looking for us but had been given our address by Maureen and was desperate to meet David and give him a present. People's generosity and kindness really struck me and I felt I was taking things in my stride and doing well.

From the beginning I was very organised. I have always been a neurotic, minimalist type of person and having a baby hadn't changed this aspect of me. Junkanoo's changing bag was always ready. It even had different compartments for different things so everything was nice and orderly. I knew exactly where to find the goodies at all times, so like well-trained boy scouts we were always prepared for any eventuality that might come our way.

<u>Things I keep in the main bit of the changing bag:</u>

- Changing mat
- Muslin
- Baby grow (for emergency change of clothes)
- Nappies
- Wet wipes
- Bottom cream (for David or me!)
- Nappy bags
- Bib
- Blanket
- Travel high chair (<u>www.totseat.com</u>)
- Hand sanitizer
- Bottle pouch - I like to think this is for keeping wine cool but I think it's meant to be for keeping the milk warm!

<u>Things I keep in a little bag in the changing bag, ready to take out if I ever go out without David or if someone else takes him out:</u>

- Lip gloss
- Lip balm
- Hand sanitizer
- Mouth freshener (you never know)
- Mirror
- Tea bag
- Diary

<u>Things I keep in the left hand end of the changing bag for easy access:</u>

- Wallet
- Phone

<u>Things I keep in the right hand end of the changing bag for emergency use:</u>

- Sachet of Calpol
- Thermometer
- Spoon (in a little case)
- Dummy (in a little case with the spoon)

One Sunday Duncan's parents, Bruce and Marie, came to see us for lunch and we walked a little way to a local restaurant. David was so good. His grandparents doted on him and it was lovely to see how delighted they looked and how proud of their son and grandson they were. On the way back though, catastrophe struck. I suddenly needed the loo, couldn't hold it in and out it came while I was walking along. I had felt an urge quite quickly and had no control whatsoever. It was one of the most humiliating experiences I have suffered.

All too soon the day came when Duncan was due to go back to work. Surprisingly I wasn't actually filled with dread or terrified about suddenly being on my own. I was feeling relatively positive and so relieved that "the baby blues" hadn't made an appearance. I seemed to be coping.

I even managed to drive to Southampton, a couple of hours away, with just the Junkanoo to navigate. It was my sister's graduation ceremony. I was very pleased with myself for managing this journey, especially as a) Junkanoo was sick all over himself in his car seat and I had to change him in a services on the M3 and b) it was raining so heavily the traffic was practically at a standstill for most of the journey.

One thing that really helped in those early days was when my cousin, Susanna, came round to visit. She was really thoughtful and caring and always insisted that I go and catch up on some sleep while she looked after Junkanoo. I'm not sure whether this was because I was too dull to be with or she wanted David to herself (!), but either way, it was so helpful and made a difference.

5

BUNDLE OF JOY MY ****

I can't remember much of the time after Duncan went back to work as it just passed in a haze. At the end of the day we would sit down at the dining room table to eat dinner and my head would be about 4 cm from the plate, such was the effort to lift the fork to my mouth. I could barely utter a word and sometimes I thought I would fall asleep in my food.

Without Duncan at home to help with the running of the house, my OCD tendencies started to get the better of me. I tried not to feel compelled to do all the jobs as soon as they needed doing, not to put things in the dishwasher as soon as they had been used, not to clean the kitchen surfaces, not to do the ironing, not to feel I had to cook a delicious meal, not to look at my emails and feel I had to reply to them immediately, but I found it incredibly hard. It even got to the point when I didn't want to receive any more cards or presents because I put pressure on myself not only to write a thank you letter immediately and then go to post it straight away, but also to write down every present in David's baby journal to look at in the future. Each day I would write a list of things to get done that day and I couldn't stop until they were all done. This way I knew I was on top of things and had some control over what was happening around me.

I found it very hard trying to do everything as I had before, to get on with life, run the house *and* look after a baby. There simply wasn't time in the day. I had expected to be able to carry on as normal and that the Junkanoo would fit in with me but this was not the case. My whole day and night, twenty four seven, were devoted to him. He couldn't do anything for himself. I had to do everything. Wherever I went, he had to go too. Whenever he wanted something, I had to try to work out what it was. Whenever he cried I had to decide whether it was serious. At the same time of course I had to boil water for bottles, wash bottles, sterilise bottles, do the shopping, cooking, cleaning, washing, putting washing out, bringing washing in, ironing, loading the dishwasher, unloading the dishwasher, personal admin. It was just a never-ending cycle of monotony. Duncan told me my expectations of myself were too high but I didn't want to have to lower them because of a baby and I could slowly see them start to slip out of my reach.

This was the time I began to hate my life. I couldn't see the point in my existence. Why was I here? Everyone would have been better off without me. Everything was so mundane, so tedious, so repetitive, nothing different or stimulating. Junkanoo and me, an empty existence. I was desperate to have some sort of self-worth, some sort of life, maybe go to a class or two to meet other mothers, but they only took place during term time. No good for me when it was the middle of July. I would have to wait until September and this seemed like an age, years away. I didn't even know if I could hold out that long.

Friends called to see how I was doing, on the landline and on my mobile, but I couldn't face talking to them. I never answered the phone at home and I turned my mobile onto silent so I didn't have to speak to anyone. The only people I felt I could talk to were my parents and my sister as I could be myself with them and not have to put on an act and pretend I was happy. I listened to people's messages and felt empty. Why were they so positive and pleased for us when I felt negative and desperate? Even the cards that were up all around the house didn't make me smile, "bundle of joy" - my ***. I wasn't cut out for this motherhood thing and I wasn't enjoying it. I felt like I had made the biggest mistake of my life.

Our sex life was deteriorating, not surprisingly, which made me very sad and confused me, although whilst writing this book I found a quote by the British author, David Lodge, which made me smile, as it sums it up perfectly: "Literature is mostly about having sex and not much about having children. Life is the other way round".

I thought I was going mad, that my life was spiralling out of control and there was nothing I could do about it. To convince myself that underneath the confusion I was actually normal, something at the back of my mind registered that when I was pregnant I had cut out a check list for symptoms of postnatal depression from a magazine and put it somewhere safe. I searched for this list diligently, almost in a frenzy, finally locating it in amongst the baby books. I looked at the checklist for the signs. I had the lot.

- ✓ Feeling low
- ✓ Feeling tearful for no apparent reason
- ✓ Irritable
- ✓ Unable to enjoy yourself
- ✓ Not wanting to leave the house
- ✓ Unable to laugh
- ✓ Finding it hard to talk
- ✓ Lacking energy
- ✓ Feeling anxious
- ✓ Feeling overwhelmed
- ✓ Lack of motivation
- ✓ Feelings of guilt
- ✓ Feelings of inadequacy
- ✓ Poor concentration
- ✓ Feeling unable to cope
- ✓ Not able to make decisions
- ✓ No interest in sex

It was a relief to know that there was actually something wrong with me, that I wasn't imagining it and I was not some psychotic person who should be locked up and the key thrown away. I phoned the local team of health visitors and suggested I might be depressed. Ruth, one of the health visitors I hadn't met before, popped round to the house that afternoon and I burst into tears on her. I filled in some questionnaire she was obliged to give me to see if I had postnatal depression and funnily enough it said that I did. She said she would arrange an emergency appointment with the doctor the next day on my behalf and phone me to let me know the time.

I waited and waited but didn't hear from Ruth. For the first time in ages I actually checked the landline and my mobile for messages but nothing. I was beginning to despair and feel panicky when the front doorbell rang. It was the health visitor, Ruth. As it turned out, she had left messages on my *old* mobile number which I had never received and when she hadn't heard from me she had driven round to the house as she was worried. She scooped me up in her arms and would have taken me to my appointment herself if she had had a car seat for David. She was so caring and it was her day off too. She had well and truly gone above and beyond the call of duty and I felt indebted to her.

The doctor prescribed antidepressants, booked an appointment in a week's time to see how I was doing and suggested I see a counsellor. I was up for anything that might make me better. I just wanted to feel like my old self again, like a human being, to be able to live life to the full rather than feeling it was passing me by. Most of all, I desperately wanted to enjoy my baby. When I got home I texted the counsellor as I didn't feel able to call and speak but unfortunately he was on holiday for the month of August. He said if I still needed to see him in

September I should book an appointment then. I made a note in my diary, just in case I might not be feeling better.

That evening, Duncan phoned his parents and my parents to tell them what was happening as both sets had been concerned but didn't want to intrude in our life. I had an overwhelming urge to be put into a hospital or even a convent and just left there by myself. That way I could lie in bed under the blankets, stare into space and not have to speak to anyone or do anything.

This would have been perfect but it wasn't possible so the next option was the parents. My parents were off to France for a month the following day so wouldn't be able to look after David or me without making lots of rearrangements - although Mum did of course say she would happily stay behind and come over as I was more important than a holiday. Duncan's Dad, Bruce, fortunately was in a position to be able to bring Marie, Duncan's Mum, over that evening and she kindly reorganised her diary to stay for the week with us and take over.

Not having to be in charge of anything or think about anything was such a relief. I felt I was safe. I spent all my time in bed. Marie did *everything* until Duncan came home each day, when I would come downstairs, have something to eat, read David a story and feed him before bed if I felt up to it and then go to bed again myself. I felt secure in our bedroom, under the duvet, away from the world. I couldn't face leaving the house and didn't go out or speak to anyone. I couldn't concentrate on television or reading so I mostly either slept or just lay there staring out of the window, looking at the sky.

Duncan had contacted my friends and told them I was suffering with postnatal depression - I didn't want them to think I was rude and ignoring them. I preferred them to know what was wrong so they could support me as and when I needed help or I could ask for it. In the middle of the week, Nikki came to see me. Although I only managed to talk - in the loosest sense of the word - to her for half an hour or so as making conversation was still too much to deal with, somewhere inside me I felt a warmth in knowing my friends had not written me off, that they did still care.

That Friday my mother-in-law, Marie, took me to my doctor's appointment at the local surgery to see how I was doing. I was still feeling pretty grim and looking pretty grim. I hadn't got dressed or left the house all week and it was a huge and daunting step to go out. Whilst in the waiting room there was a lady, Sharon, talking to people about an organisation called "Sure Start", a government initiative run by local authorities. I couldn't really focus on what she was saying and when she came to speak to me I started to cry. I felt such a fool in front of all the other people, mothers who were clearly loving having little babies, crying my eyes out for no apparent reason. I just wanted to be swallowed up by the sofa and never see anyone ever again as it seemed everyone must be looking at me, judging me and feeling sorry for me.

When I was called in for my appointment I was still in floods of tears so things obviously weren't getting better yet. I couldn't wait for things to improve and I would have given anything for it to happen there and then. The doctor was very sympathetic about the postnatal depression although when I had pulled myself together enough to mention the bowel incontinence, his only suggestion was to take Immodium. I was rather surprised by this remedial action but who was I to question his knowledge and authority?

Not losing the baby weight I had put on didn't help my self-esteem much either. I had expected it to fall off really quickly but I was still wearing my maternity clothes or pyjamas every day as nothing else fitted me by a long shot. Duncan was really kind and kept saying "nine months on, nine months off", reiterating that he still found me attractive and even if I was never a size 8 again, he loved me unfailingly. Right things to say, Duncan, well done.

6

I'M A MOTHER - GET ME OUT OF HERE!

It was decided that I would go out to France earlier than planned so I could stay with my parents for several weeks and they could look after David and me. This seemed the logical solution as Marie had to get back home to Bruce and Duncan wasn't able to take time off work immediately. He would join us in France later. At the time I was so unaware of anything going on around me and felt so zombie-like in my own little bubble that the prospect of travelling to France by myself with a 6 week old baby didn't really phase me. It didn't occur to me that it could be stressful or difficult. All I could think about was seeing my Mum and Dad and being safe, being looked after and switching off. The thought of not having to look after David or take responsibility for him was heaven.

Somehow, at my lowest, I still managed the practical task of packing for Junkanoo, even though it took me hours because it was so hard to think straight and stay focused. I have never seen so much paraphernalia in one suitcase:

<u>Things Junkanoo needs for an overnight stay</u>

- Muslins x 1 per day
- Babygrow x 2 per day (one for bed time, one in case of emergency)
- Outfit x 1 per day
- Milk formula
- Milk bottles
- Bottle brush
- Sterilizer bags (need microwave)
- Nappies
- Wet wipes
- Wash bag containing miniature toothbrush, toothpaste, sun cream, bubble bath
- Sheet
- Grow bag
- A couple of small toys
- Travel cot
- Push chair
- Car seat

Duncan dropped me off at the airport and helped with all the bits and bobs and then we had to say goodbye. I was still sad and empty but Duncan assured me that when we next saw each other I would be feeling a bit better. I was silently and inwardly hopeful.

Going through the security checks was a nightmare. I can't begin to describe how awful it was. First of all, I saw the sign saying that any liquids over a certain amount would be confiscated and all I could think of was Junkanoo's thousands of milk bottles in my changing bag. I started having a panic attack although I tried to keep myself under control to avoid stares from the people around me. Then I saw a sign saying all liquids needed to be in a clear plastic bag and I didn't have one. I started shaking and then I began to cry.

By the time I got to the front of the queue and it was my turn to go through the security checks I was a complete and utter wreck - what a sight I must have been. I had no idea how I was going to get David out of the push chair, fold it up, put it through the scanner, show all my milk bottles, take off my shoes, hold David etc. etc. and I was rooted to the spot with fear. Luckily for me one of the security men saw that all was not right (in my mind!), closed off one of the lanes, cuddled David for me and helped me out. He was so understanding and I was so grateful. Looking back on this always brings a tear to my eye as even though I was at rock bottom, people were understanding and helped me, even strangers.

Being in France with Mum and Dad was exactly what I needed. They let me rest and looked after me and I could be myself: sleeping, talking, getting up, doing things when I felt I could. There was no pressure to do anything I couldn't face and they took control as if I were a little girl again. Occasionally I was brave enough to go out with them and as the days went by

I think I managed to do more things, although I was still quiet and withdrawn.

My Auntie Gillian came out to stay too and she helped look after David as well, her speciality being the nightly eleven o'clock feed. I was doing the three in the morning feed and didn't mind doing this because it was about all I was doing . . .

Finally, after many days blurring into one, Duncan arrived. I was so pleased to see him and for us to be together. It was delightful being cuddled and reassured that he still loved me. We spent our time relaxing and I started to feel a bit more like going outside. We even went swimming in a neighbour's pool one afternoon, all of us, Junkanoo included, and that is when I laughed. It was a startling noise for everyone, especially me, because I hadn't laughed for a very long time. Mum and Duncan cast side-long glances at each other and I couldn't believe it. I had to keep telling myself "I laughed, I laughed, I am going to be OK, I am going to be OK". This was the beginning of the end, finally.

7

SINK OR SWIM

Very very slowly, things started to improve although there were still more bad times than good. I desperately wanted to get better and I wanted it to happen overnight (I am a very impatient person) but I knew it wouldn't, that it was a long haul and I had to take things slowly.

I didn't make myself do things I didn't want to and I lived from day to day, not focusing on the future, but making it through the present. I am a fan of the current Dalai Lama whom I met once when I was air-hostessing on a Brussels to Heathrow early morning flight. He shook my hand and I have never felt such an aura of positive energy around a person. He would definitely have approved of this fantastic quote from Buddha which summed up what I was trying to do:

"Do not dwell in the past, do not dream of the future, concentrate the mind on the present moment".

This is how I started to get onto the right tracks, by taking things steadily and making adjustments along the way.

I had always liked reading as opposed to watching television and I hadn't read anything in ages as I simply didn't have the concentration span or brain capacity. One day I decided I was feeling brave enough to try this pastime again. I started with magazines: magazines of any variety, even if I wasn't interested in the content, because they had manageable, short-length articles that I could read without my brain frazzling.

Once back in England, I was fending for myself again and although I was no longer in the depths of despair, I was still finding it very hard to cope and stay afloat. Duncan and I discussed how we could tackle this and we started chatting about employing an au pair - a nanny wasn't really within our budget. The more we discussed it, the more this seemed like the perfect solution and I wrote a list of the pros and cons to help with our decision making:

<u>Pros</u>

- ❖ A break for me from David, allowing some "me" time
- ❖ Company for me during the day and evening as Duncan goes to work early and gets back late
- ❖ Babysitting part of contract and included in price
- ❖ Cheap (minimum £35 per week)
- ❖ Someone to help with the cleaning
- ❖ Someone to iron Duncan's shirts - my most loathed job in the world
- ❖ Cultural exchange for all involved

<u>Cons</u>

- Sharing the house with a stranger
- Increased food bills
- Potential for nightmare scenarios (trashing house, stealing things, abusing child, clashing personalities)

We lost no time in looking on websites. Duncan's boss recommended one and he and his wife have had at least three au pairs! We came up with a short list of five potential candidates. I say "we" but it was actually Duncan. I had very little input as I was still not able to focus or concentrate and couldn't take it all in.

Some people weren't so enthusiastic about our idea though. They didn't hesitate to tell us that they considered having an au pair to be a cardinal sin, tantamount to abandoning your child to be brought up by someone else because you don't care for it. This opinion was one I chose to ignore and I found it unhelpful at a time when I was trying to get my life back on track.

One weekend Duncan and I ventured forth to a summer BBQ at Karl and Tracy's house, Duncan's best friend and his wife. It was the first time that lots of the people there had met Junkanoo and they all had a stream of questions and were so excited. I had warned Duncan that I didn't think I was ready to face the crowds just yet and he was brilliant. He said he wouldn't leave my side for a minute and that he would look after me so I wouldn't be on my own having to field everyone's questions.

Duncan actually did most of the talking as this was something I still found hard and which required a lot of effort. As the evening wore on I felt increasingly like an outsider, an abnormal mother who would prefer not to have a baby, someone who wasn't enjoying motherhood and didn't want to talk about it. All I wanted to do was lie down and hide in a dark room. I tried to put on a brave face, smile and display a front of motherly joy but failed miserably. People didn't really know what to do or say so the easiest thing for all concerned was for me to take myself away and go to bed.

The only good thing to come out of the BBQ was seeing the wife of one of Duncan's old friends again, Lucy. I had met her a couple of years before at a party she and her husband had thrown but hadn't actually chatted to her that much and consequently hadn't got to know her. Talking to her in the garden at around six in the morning (David was up and so were her girls), she mentioned that she had recently separated from her husband and had been finding things hard, particularly looking after her children by herself. I warmed to her immediately and although I was sad for her current situation, in a perverse way it was nice to know I wasn't the only one feeling glum. I felt that she was someone who might understand me and take me seriously. The two of us talked honestly and openly to each other and it helped that I could be myself and didn't have to pretend I was alright. I took her number and said that if it fitted in with her, maybe Duncan, David and I could come and stay with her one weekend for a break. If you don't ask you don't get and luckily Lucy didn't seem too aghast at my forward suggestion.

Naturally during this time there were occasions when we were on the receiving end of well-meaning advice. It made me furious. Not at any stage since David's birth had Duncan and I not talked about how to bring him up and do what we regarded to be the right thing. We had discussed all sorts of different ideas / methods / ways of doing things and ultimately chosen to do what we deemed best. If it didn't work, we tried something different as we considered we were both intelligent adults with the capacity to make sensible decisions for ourselves. David was only a couple of months old but not a day had gone by when he hadn't been cared for to the best of our ability, loved and cherished. Even in the depths of depression, David was looked after and wanted for nothing.

Eventually when my anger had subsided, I decided these drastic times called for drastic measures: I would have my hair done. For it to have any style at all I needed to straighten it every day and I simply didn't have time to do this with a little baby to look after. It wasn't my priority. So I booked myself in at the hairdresser's and made an appointment to have the lot chopped off and some cheeky highlights put in. I treated myself and went back to the salon near our old house. Very expensive but the plan was it would make me feel good about myself and a bit special. It also gave me a break from Junkanoo as Mum looked after him for the afternoon. I was delighted with the new look. I felt more attractive and had enjoyed not having to look after David.

By this stage I had definitely expected the baby weight to have fallen off but I still had a long way to go and was *still* wearing maternity clothes and even Duncan's pyjama bottoms on really bad days when I couldn't face deciding what fat person item to wear. This was really demoralising. I had a lovely wardrobe full of beautiful clothes that were just sitting there and I was having to wear the same old maternity clothes, day in day out, when I wasn't even pregnant. I hated it.

One Saturday afternoon, the neighbours, Johnboy and Laura, were having a BBQ to which we had been invited. The day arrived bright and sunny but despite trying to rally myself to be enthusiastic, I couldn't face it. I found the prospect of mixing with people I didn't know extremely scary and overwhelming. I plucked up the courage from somewhere to pop round and tell them that only Duncan would be there and I can remember Laura asking how I was doing, as neighbours do. We didn't know each other that well and I told her how sad, alone and unhappy I was feeling. She was really surprised and upset to hear this and felt terrible that she lived next door yet had no idea. And that was the start of a great friendship. From that moment, Laura took it upon herself to keep an eye on me when Duncan was at work and would pop round to check I was alright from time to time.

Soon it was September and the baby classes I had signed up for started. By now I had been a mother for long enough to know that I had no desire to meet other mothers in order to talk about babies non-stop. This just wasn't me. My life was not - and is still not - dominated by a baby and I felt I had better things to do with my time than discuss every single aspect of babies. I was keen however to meet other mums to see how they were coping as parents, to see if their experiences were the same as mine, to see if there were other people out there who weren't finding this new life a walk in the park.

Whilst I didn't sign up for these baby classes to necessarily make new friends (I already had a good circle of friends and didn't feel a compelling desire to make new friends just because they had a baby too), I was still a bit daunted because I knew I wasn't a particularly fun person to be around. I didn't want people to think I was boring or dull because I knew that I wasn't. It was only temporary.

The first activity of the week was a Sure Start "mother and baby drop in session" in a local church hall on Monday morning. I turned up not knowing what to expect and recognised Sharon, the lady who had given me the brochure at the doctors' surgery a couple of months before. She recognised me immediately and gave me a hug, telling me how well I was looking and that she was pleased I had made it along to join in. Whilst I didn't exactly join in, and sat there quietly while everyone else chatted, I was proud of myself for getting dressed, making it out of the house and being around other people.

The second activity of the week was a swimming "lesson" on Tuesday morning. This was very near our house so I could walk there and get some fresh air. I enjoyed doing this with David. We sang some nursery rhymes and included actions in the water to go with the words. David enjoyed the swimming too and didn't cry. I felt glad to be giving him the opportunity to try something different and it was also nice to see my son with other children. I didn't really bond with any of the other parents but that wasn't why I went. I went there for David, not for me.

The third activity of the week was "mother and baby yoga" with Jessica. I turned up for this and recognised some familiar faces from the antenatal yoga group. Again, I wasn't sure how people would be and I was so taken aback, in a good way, when everyone hugged and kissed me as I couldn't believe that they were actually glad to see me and didn't see me as an outsider, the way I saw myself.

The group started the same way it always had, with Jessica asking people how they were. I was open from the beginning as I preferred people to know that I was suffering from postnatal depression and not enjoying motherhood. Not so they would feel sorry for me or pander to me, but so they knew this wasn't actually the real me and wouldn't ignore me because I wasn't chatty or happy. Nobody else was feeling as I did but everybody was kind and it didn't seem to put anyone off talking to me after the class.

The fourth activity of the week was the OAP walk. I was feeling brave when I went to this as I knew I had got through three other things that week and survived without people giving me weird looks or the cold shoulder. I was doing OK! I was a mother and I was doing OK! Everyone at the walk was delighted to see David and me and I was touched that people wanted to talk to me and to hold David afterwards - they were literally queuing up, it was really sweet. Whilst my conversation wasn't up to much, I was delighted to show off my little son to them - and rather glad that I had some respite from holding him.

I can't actually remember what I did on the Friday; maybe I had a break from David's social life. I am not sure.

One day in early September when Junkanoo was ten weeks old, Duncan booked him in for the weekend to be looked after by his parents, and us in for the weekend at a boutique hotel in Bournemouth, The Urban Beach Hotel. I was really looking forward to some time together with Duncan so we could enjoy each other's company and have a break from the stresses and strains of the world. The weekend didn't disappoint. We had cocktails on room service, watched some DVDs whilst snuggling up in bed, snoozed, went out for a walk, and had a delicious sea-food dinner on the seafront. It was fantastic to feel and behave like a normal couple.

That was the weekend too that we first contacted the girl we had chosen to be David's au pair. As before, I say the girl "we" had chosen to be David's au pair lightly, the reality of the matter being that Duncan and his office (the majority being men) had vetted all the potentials on-line and short-listed her. To this day I am still not convinced by their process of whittling the girls down to a finalist but here is a list of Matilda's attributes - oh, sorry - that should say au pair skills:

1) 18 years old
2) Blonde
3) Swedish
4) Single

So Duncan called Matilda as I was still not up to talking to people I didn't know and found it far too daunting. The conversation went well and it was decided that she would look at flights and come and live with us as soon as possible after we returned from our planned break in Mallorca at the end of September. I couldn't wait. Although I wasn't excited, I did feel it was something to look forward to, as it meant I would no longer have to cope by myself and would have help for as long as I needed it in order to recover and get my life back to some semblance of normality.

Around that time I also saw the note I had written in my diary to remind myself to contact the counsellor, should I still be in need. I thought about it carefully and decided I was doing fine without one. I knew the steps I needed to take to get better and the things I should be doing. I had read enough and to be honest, I didn't know what I would do with David during a counselling session anyway, so it kind of defeated the object.

It was mid-September that my hair started falling out and I don't mean the odd one here and there. It wasn't dissimilar to a dog moulting. There were clumps of the stuff everywhere from the bathroom floor to my pillow. Revolting. The mad pills were slowly starting to work but I was physically starting to fall apart again. I had had enough.

Our mini break to Mallorca was just what the doctor ordered. The three of us stayed with the parents of one of Duncan's longest-standing friends, Gareth, who lived out there in a beautiful villa plus infinity pool. The holiday was quiet and relaxing and nobody minded when I went for a lie down to have some time to myself. I wasn't made to feel odd. People were concerned and just wanted me to do what I had to in order to get better. Whilst we were there we even managed a little trip to the beach with David, the three of us, a little family. It was good. In small doses, with everyone's support, I could manage things, cope with life and I was getting through each day, and days were becoming weeks.

I was on the mend, definitely swimming more than sinking, although there were still weights attached to various parts of my body, both metaphorically and literally.

8

EVERY CLOUD HAS A SILVER LINING

Towards the end of September, Matilda arrived, not a moment too soon. I remember the journey to Heathrow vividly. I set the Sat Nav and off David and I went to pick up our au pair, leaving plenty of time to ensure we were there before her so she wouldn't be waiting for us. I had actually made an effort with my appearance that day, a bit of makeup and some wax in the hair because a) I was going out into the big wide world and b) I had seen Matilda's photo and she was not what you would call ugly. I was barely recognisable.

En route to the airport I drove through some dodgy outer-London areas and found a place that cut keys, just as well because one of my jobs that week had been to get a key cut for Matilda and I hadn't got round to it. I dashed in with Junkanoo tucked under one arm, had the key copied, couldn't find my purse, surrendered David to be held by the man in the shop whilst I rifled around and duly found said purse (someone had put it back in the wrong section of the changing bag), paid, then dashed off to continue our journey to Heathrow.

As David and I waited at *Arrivals*, I felt a little nervous but also relieved that I was going to have some help. I was desperate to feel normal again and get back to my "old" self. Both Duncan and I had agreed that this would be an interim measure to try and get things back to how they were and I fervently hoped that Matilda would be the answer to our prayers.

And she was a godsend. She was easy to have around the house, helpful, kind and thoughtful. It was like having a daughter or friend living with us. Right from the beginning it worked well and suited us all. To this day I think how lucky we were. It could have been awful but it wasn't. It was one of the best decisions we ever made and we were very fortunate that it worked marvellously.

The main benefits of having Matilda were:

- → she did the 7am feed so I could catch up on sleep
- → she was good company
- → she cooked some meals
- → she was always there to babysit if we wanted or needed to go out
- → she ironed Duncan's shirts
- → she looked after David while I went to the gym to train for the London Marathon

BTW, that last one is not a red herring. In a moment of madness I decided that:

a) it would be a good way to motivate myself to get fit again
b) it would be a perfect opportunity to raise money for The Children's Society. I've done sponsored walks for them before but nothing too hard-core
c) it would be a real personal achievement

And what better way to kill these three birds with one stone than running the London Marathon?

Training was slow and sporadic, although I did start to increase the distances as time progressed. The main problem was that I still had limited control of my bowel and being out and about was not ideal when I suddenly had an urge to go to the loo. There are at least five places locally that have been my "pit stops", ranging from the local curry house and off-licence to a bush by the roadside. Not attractive and certainly mortifying. There was also one time when there was absolutely nowhere I could go so I had to suffer the inevitable. Awful and humiliating and nothing I could do about it.

The yoga classes were going well and as I have said, whilst I am not a natural earth mother type, I did enjoy them as I liked the others who were there. One week, I'm not exactly sure what came over me, but at the end of the lesson I heard this voice, that sounded suspiciously like my own, invite everyone over for lunch the following week. I couldn't believe my ears and I certainly couldn't believe it was me who had said this. To my surprise and secret delight, everyone said yes straight away and seemed genuinely pleased to be meeting up. I was stunned that I had initiated something so spontaneously and this was a real sign that things were moving forward.

The day before the yoga girls were coming round for lunch I had no idea what to cook. My mind went blank as I didn't want anything that took too long to prepare but I also wanted to do something nice for everyone so they might think about coming back. So I sat down, thought about it and decided to write down a list of meals I knew how to cook without a recipe book. Not only would this help me decide the meal for the next day, I could put it up on the fridge to refer to at times I needed inspiration. Parfait!

<u>Simple Meals I know I can cook without a recipe book</u>

- Salmon and scrambled eggs on toast
- Spanish omelette
- Bolognaise sauce
- Carbonara sauce
- Curry
- Stuffed chicken breast wrapped in Parma ham
- Toasted sandwiches
- Full English breakfast
- Beans on toast

- Chicken fajitas
- Bangers and mash with gravy
- Meatballs in tomato sauce
- Fisherman's pie
- Braising steak with dumplings
- Lasagne
- Fish (fingers) and chips
- Cauliflower cheese
- Green soup (broccoli and blue cheese)
- Orange soup (carrot and coriander)
- Pork stroganoff
- Quiche
- Steak
- Risotto (various)
- Pumpkin soup
- Butternut squash soup
- Stir fry
- Chinese chicken noodles
- Moussaka

I made soup and sandwiches that day and the yoga lunch was a success. Everyone came round with their babies and we were able to sit outside as it was such a glorious day. I have to say I enjoyed myself and I might even go as far as to say I was a smiley and decent hostess. I also felt very pleased with myself for managing to host a lunch, albeit small and simple, having people round and taking the situation in hand. This was the time I realised I might have made some new friends who actually liked me. My confidence had a direct boost and I actually felt good about myself.

It was at the three month point that I had my epiphany and actually realised I was a mother, that I had a baby who I loved and who loved me. The penny finally dropped and I started accepting my new life for what it was. I was still finding it very hard. There was no doubt about that, but I felt I was making progress, especially as David became a little person rather than a little thing. Just seeing him smile, move or look around was the most wonderful thing and I began to see the good in life once more. I cried and cried, thankful that I wasn't mad. I wasn't a misery all the time and I had hope, hope that my life would improve and I would be the person I used to be.

David, Matilda and I were invited to a local coffee morning not long after she moved in with us so we thought we'd give it a go. Off we went, for our little outing, not at all sure what it would be like, and I have to say I will not be going to another. Although I hadn't particularly been enjoying my life it made me realise that I certainly didn't want to spend it sitting around drinking tea and coffee and talking about other people. For me, life is for the taking and I need to get out there and take it!

This revelation that I was a mother with a baby led nicely onto a weekend at Lucy's in Herefordshire - no coffee involved but lots of wine. Although it took us a while to get there it was well worth it because once there I could relax and be myself. Lucy's children even had some friends over for a little party on the Saturday and I didn't feel the need to go and hide. I actually joined in and helped organise some games.

Unbelievable. I was on the mend and feeling happier in myself and more talkative again. Such relief.

One Monday at one of the baby weigh-in sessions there was a lady I had seen before but had never spoken to. She looked very vacant that particular day and I made myself go and speak to her. Her name was Charlie and she burst into tears on me and poured her heart out. As it happened, she was experiencing all the same feelings that I had had and was feeling low too. I believe in fate and I am sure we were meant to talk to each other. I had a use that day, someone needed me and I could help by talking to them so they didn't feel alone. I felt stronger than I had in ages and positive too that I could perhaps make a difference to someone else in their time of need, like so many people had to me. I was starting to be able to give something back to society and it was good.

As things were gradually improving, I was definitely ready for another spa weekend with my friends Van and Laura, so accordingly they organised one. We had a really relaxing time and it was great being without David for the whole weekend. I could get away from my life of having a baby and actually be normal, like a grown up, like an adult who has a life. We chatted, ate delicious food, had some treatments and lounged in the bedroom with face masks on whilst drinking pink fizz. It seemed so decadent and a million miles away from reality. I loved it.

That was when fate struck again and I read a magazine article in one of the monthlies that the girls had brought with them. It was about one woman's reaction to having a baby. I read it without saying a word. It was almost as if the author knew all my inner feelings and had put them down on paper as her own. It was quite a shock but very thought-provoking. After over half a year trying to work out what was wrong with me, there it was, beautifully summed up in this article: "I don't enjoy being a full time Mum". I felt as if I had been thunderstruck and had to read the article over and over again. There was someone out there after all who was like me. I was relieved to know this and it also inspired me to take action and think about returning to work.

Returning to work within the year's maternity leave was not something I had considered. Before David's arrival I had always assumed I would take off at least the year and possibly never return to work, but this couldn't have been further from my thoughts at this time. Going back to my old job was not an option due to our new location so there was no immediate ball I could set rolling. I did update my CV though and kept my ear to the ground as to what I could do locally. I wasn't particularly fussy. I just wanted a job to get me out of the house, to let me have a break from David, to give me some self-worth and some money that I had earned myself.

As it happened, work was right on my doorstep. Through a casual conversation with a lady, Sue, whom I had met at yoga, I started working part-time as an Events Manager at a company which she had set up herself. I was genuinely excited, firstly about working again and secondly that someone had seen something in me they thought was promising. It boosted my confidence and made me feel valued and capable and that I could do things other than look after a baby.

Starting work was a turning point for me. I could dedicate my mornings to David and enjoy him growing up and then work in the afternoon while Matilda looked after him. This routine worked brilliantly. It gave me a good work-life balance as it allowed me to enjoy Junkanoo *and* my job and enabled me to put my best into both for optimum results.

Most people were supportive of me working and having time away from David, although I do recall one lady I met commenting "don't you think that's a bit ambitious?" when I told her about my job in the afternoons. Oh well, you can't please everyone, and I realised then that some people do actually believe a woman's place is in the home bringing up children and doing nothing else. Certainly not the life for me.

Although I was a lot better, things had unsurprisingly been strained at times between Duncan and me. Having a child is the most difficult thing I have ever done and I've often thought that if we were not married then we would not be together now. At times I had to force myself to remember our marriage vows, that the two of us are the most important thing in the family unit, and thinking of our promises to each other did keep me going. I would remember why I loved Duncan and that I had vowed to be with him through the good and the bad. We had definitely had enough of the bad so I tried to focus on the good, like Christmas and our approaching wedding anniversary.

The 21st December arrived, the day of our wedding anniversary. Mum and Dad were going to look after David for the night so Duncan and I could go out for a romantic getaway. We had booked a table and a room for the night at a lovely local hotel to spend some time just the two of us, to focus on each other. Unfortunately we never made it to the hotel due to severe snow and weather conditions and consequently we ended up staying at Mum and Dad's little cottage for the night instead. Not the romantic evening we had envisaged but it was cosy as we slept on the floor in front of the fire in their sitting room.

There is a moral to the story: always have emergency rations in the car for a journey as you never know how long it might take. A journey that should have taken 1 ½ hours ended up taking 4 and we didn't have any milk or food in the car for David.

Emergency rations hidden in car

- Milk formula cartons x 3
- Packet of rusks

- Miniature champagne bottles x 2 (not for David's consumption)

Christmas and New Year's Eve came and went. I found these "celebrations" quite hard as I wasn't yet up to celebrating. Admittedly things were a lot better but life was still difficult and it was a struggle coming to terms with being a mother.

What I could see clearly though was a light at the end of the tunnel. I couldn't reach it and I was some distance from it, but it was there and in it I could see Duncan, a silhouette, reaching to pull me into sunshine and a fulfilling life together with our son, David. Although he was only a silhouette I knew he had a smile on his face and loved me.

9

NEW YEAR, NEW ME

<u>Top Tips I try to remember for my survival and sanity:</u>

- I need to care for myself. If I am OK, everyone else will be
- Try to get out of the house at least once a day
- Don't put too much in the diary
- Don't have a "to do" list. If something doesn't get done, it wasn't that important and can be done another day
- Have a lie down if it is needed (and possible), everything else can wait
- Don't expect to get much done with a baby that's awake.
- Have one task to achieve each day and gradually increase this
- Have a list of meals I know I can cook on the fridge door
- Always save a couple of baby-size portions of food when cooking, for the next day or for the freezer, so there is always a meal ready and I am never stuck for ideas or time

- Remind myself that it is not out of the norm for a child to go to a nursery / child minder / have a nanny / au pair (if finances permit)
- Listen to other people's "advice" and feel free to accept it or not
- Do what I believe is right for our family
- Have a list handy of things to pack for baby when going away
- Have the changing bag ready to go at all times

So, six months after David was born I was on the mend and decided to take action about my looks and have laser eye surgery. It was something I had thought about for a while on and off and several friends had had it done with excellent results so I made up my mind to take the plunge. It was possibly more painful than childbirth but the results were indeed excellent and I was delighted - no more glasses and feeling "square". I started wearing make up more often as I felt it could be seen and was no longer hidden behind spectacles and I started to make a bit more of an effort with my appearance in general. This was another boost for my self-esteem as well as an excuse to go and buy some designer sunglasses, very exciting.

I had finally lost a bit of baby weight and my fitness regime was going well too. I was not as fit as I had been pre-baby but I was certainly no couch potato. Laura next door had taken me under her wing as she was an expert when it came to running due to her avid reading of "Runners' World" magazine. She had plenty of tips and pointers and she lost no time in signing us up for the Bath Half Marathon in February, husbands included. When we were not drinking pink fizz, we could often be seen pounding the streets with Junkanoo in his running buggy and one of us pushing him - usually Laura up the hills - much to the admiration of passers-by.

The "Bath Half" was brilliant and I was delighted to have completed it. Of course it was great to have Laura, Johnboy and Duncan running the race as well for some moral support, but the most important thing to me was to make Duncan proud of me, which he certainly was.

That March we went on holiday to the States to stay with some American friends, Chad and Sabrina, who have five children - yes, five. We had a fantastic break and although I had originally been slightly daunted at the prospect of being around so many children, we had a whale of a time and I loved being with them and playing, just like I had always done. Things were becoming so much better and I think we fitted in because we were a cohesive family unit, despite my occasional, and probably irrational, doubts.

By now it was time for Matilda to leave. She was ready and so were we, and I was feeling positive. Before she went she asked me to write a reference for her which I readily did. After all, she helped my through one of the darkest patches of my life and a lot of my recovery was due to her being there for me, every day, for over half a year. This is what I wrote:

Matilda lived with us for seven months and we thoroughly enjoyed having her with us. She settled in and became a member of our family very quickly due to her friendly disposition, outgoing nature and great sense of humour.

Although Matilda had not looked after a baby before, she rose to the challenge and was quick to learn; she carried out her responsibilities both positively and professionally.

I would say that Matilda's best qualities are her honesty, reliability and resourcefulness as these make her a trustworthy, responsible and dependable young lady.

We found it very useful that she was flexible, organised and hard-working in her approach to her job, as well as being very kind by nature.

Her English is superb and she has made considerable improvement since she arrived.

We will miss her and she will be an asset to her next employer.

So now to life with me taking control of the reins. An exciting but slightly alarming prospect, considering I hadn't felt in control of anything for a very long time and now it was just me, myself and I.

It was action stations straight away. I embraced my time spent with David as heartily as I could, taking things slowly but surely. We went to two signing classes per week, one which was run by Sure Start and was free and another which cost more but was equally fun. We visited zoos and farms where David could see and sometimes touch all the animals if they hadn't run away from him in fear. We went to a new swimming group which actually taught babies to swim as supposed to them just being held in the water and swooshed around to nursery rhymes, a proper big boy class.

I also continued to make an effort with my appearance. I had my hair highlighted, used my epilator, having taken it out from the back of the wardrobe and dusted it off, and had my eyebrows waxed and tinted. In short, the feminine things I hadn't done for ages as I had previously felt too ugly and disgusting to justify doing them.

At this time David started going to a child minder every afternoon, which he thoroughly enjoyed, so I could carry on with my work and train for the marathon. This suited us perfectly, a win win situation for both of us to have time apart and quality time together.

Talking about winning things, although I didn't win the London Marathon, not even a close second, I completed it in just under 5 ½ hours, a real personal achievement 9 months after giving birth. Only one emergency loo stop too - progress. My parents, sister, Duncan, David and Leon, one of Duncan's friends, turned out to support me on my big day and I have to say that I think Duncan, with David on his back, might have run as far as me in his quest to cheer me on at as many places en route as possible. I also managed to raise just over £1,600 for The Children's Society so all in all, a good day's running.

10

LIFE IN THE FAST LANE

After David's first birthday life was much better and I was generally on top of things. Finally. I even went out and about and didn't have to pretend I was enjoying myself because I actually was. A miracle. My social life started to pick up and some might even have said I was getting around.

One morning at a signing class, I wondered why the teacher had made a special effort with her appearance and was wearing a pretty dress and leggings. The reason soon became apparent when she announced to us that Natalie Cassidy of Eastenders and Strictly Come Dancing fame was coming along to the class to be filmed with some of the babies for a one-off programme to be aired on television the following week. I soon got over the fact I had no makeup on and told myself to be thankful that I wasn't in my pyjamas. Whilst I am not a particular fan, it was a great morning and I felt full of nervous energy, buzzing, much like my old self.

In the evenings I often found myself drawn to watching documentaries featuring children of various ages from different countries and backgrounds.

One documentary in particular featured children in Ethiopia with a little-heard-of disease called 'Noma' which eats away at children's faces and can leave them severely disfigured literally with big gaps in their faces. It showed how this affects their lives, with those afflicted sometimes even being abandoned by their families. I find watching this sort of programme heart-breaking but compelling, as every time it makes me think how much we take for granted in our Western civilisation. Seeing these children who have such severe disfigurements yet are uncomplainingly stoical always makes me put things in perspective and realise just how fortunate I am to have a healthy, happy baby. This way, when I think I am having a bad day, it fades into insignificance, as who am I to feel sorry for myself when I want for nothing?

One afternoon we went for an adventure as a family to the local park. To my delight the babies' paddling pool was open for the summer, full of water with children running around in their swimming costumes - the ones with prepared parents - and underwear - the ones with unprepared parents. I couldn't wait to get in there with David and quickly stripped him down to his nappy before we waded in to have a paddle. It was great! Duncan spectated from the side-lines, ostensibly to keep an eye on our things but really because he didn't want to get splashed by the children running around with water pistols, while David crawled and walked with me by his side. After a while Duncan came to join us. I think he wanted to be part of our fun. He told me how lovely it was to see me with our son, that I am a wonderful mother whom David adores and how much he enjoyed watching us just be happy and laughing together.

One of the final successes in my first year as a mother was hosting a little dinner party for my new baby friends. Yes, that's right, friends, not just people I met who have babies too, but friends. It finally just "happened", nothing was forced, we simply found that we enjoyed each other's company and it didn't have to revolve around babies.

We also made a big decision to get a rescue dog, a beautiful German Shepherd called Star, who quickly established herself as a member of the family, or perhaps that should say, as David's partner in crime, since he takes great delight in taking things out of cupboards and off shelves and giving them to her to chew or eat. Between the two of them there is never a dull moment . . .

11

THE LIGHT AT THE END OF THE TUNNEL

Nothing had prepared me for what it was like to be a mother. I had read the books, spoken to lots of people, expected to feel exhausted and emotional but I had no idea how completely life-changing it would be. I had always expected to take to it like a duck to water and no other scenario had crossed my mind. I had the perfect picture in my head of the perfect family, all white-toothed smiles and classic clothes, lustrous hair and not a care in the world, living a wonderful, harmonious life and enjoying every second to the max. How let down I had been when it finally dawned on me that this was not most people's reality.

I thought I would never see the day when I was happy and enjoyed being a mother and having a baby. But I was wrong; things really are on the up. I think I might even be out of the tunnel and standing in the light but I don't want to overdo it or speak too soon.

I still have my moments of madness though. One evening for example, my husband and I went out with a group of friends to a local restaurant. On returning home, I thought it would be a lovely idea for us both to walk the babysitter home as it was such a warm evening. It was only as I was changing out of my beautiful sparkly heels into something more appropriate for a jaunt through the fields that Duncan suggested perhaps one of us should not go after all, as there should really be an adult in the house with the baby. How slow am I?

It would be an understatement to say that motherhood has taken a while to sink in and even now I'm not sure that it has completely, but ultimately I'm a mother and I have a baby, and not only that, I'm a good mother.

So is there life after baby? Yes, definitely, although it has taken me a while to find it, get the balance right and embrace it. I have gone through the mother of all journeys and life will never be the same: it's not better, it's not worse, it's different, and with the help and love of husband, friends and family I am making every effort to live it to the best of my ability and overcome the hurdles I encounter. As Jean-Paul Sartre so correctly sums it up, "everything has been figured out, except how to live".

<u>INSPIRATIONAL QUOTES</u>

I came across these quotes as I was writing the book and in their different ways they spoke to me about my journey to motherhood. Whilst there was no particular place for them in the main body of the text I thought they were very apt and too good to leave out.

Life consists not in holding good cards but in playing those you hold well. - Josh Billings

My formula for living is quite simple. I get up in the morning and I go to bed at night. In between, I occupy myself as best I can. - Cary Grant

Any idiot can face a crisis - it's day to day living that wears you out. - Anton Chekhov

It's not easy being a mother. If it were easy, fathers would do it. - From "The Golden Girls"

God could not be everywhere, so he created mothers. - Jewish Proverb

If evolution really works, how come mothers only have two hands? - Milton Berle

There is no way to be a perfect mother, and a million ways to be a good one. - Jill Churchill

ACKNOWLEDGEMENTS

I would like to thank my Mum and Duncan for reading the first draft and giving me their honest thoughts, opinions and ideas. An especially large thank you goes to my uncle for giving up his spare time to painstakingly edit my work xxx

<u>www.themotherofalljourneys.co.uk</u>

CPSIA information can be obtained at www.ICGtesting.com
Printed in the USA
LVOW101909080412

276659LV00006B/4/P